DISCARD

How to Draw The Best of NICKELODEON

Hey Nick Fans,

Stop channel surfing and get ready to draw the best of the best from Nick's cartoon lineup! From SpongeBob to Jimmy and Timmy to Tommy, this book is chock-full of all your favorite animated characters. And inside you'll find tons of hints and tips to help you draw like the pros. So grab some paper and sharpen your skills (and your pencil). Oh, and turn this page to get started!

With illustrations by Steve Crespo, Heather Martinez, and Gregg Schigiel

Shape Starter

Everything around us is made up of shapes. Below are some different examples. Before you draw, look closely to find the basic shapes that make up each character in this book. Then just follow the illustrated steps. As you draw, the shapes will come together to create people, fairies, and even underwater heroes!

CIRCLE

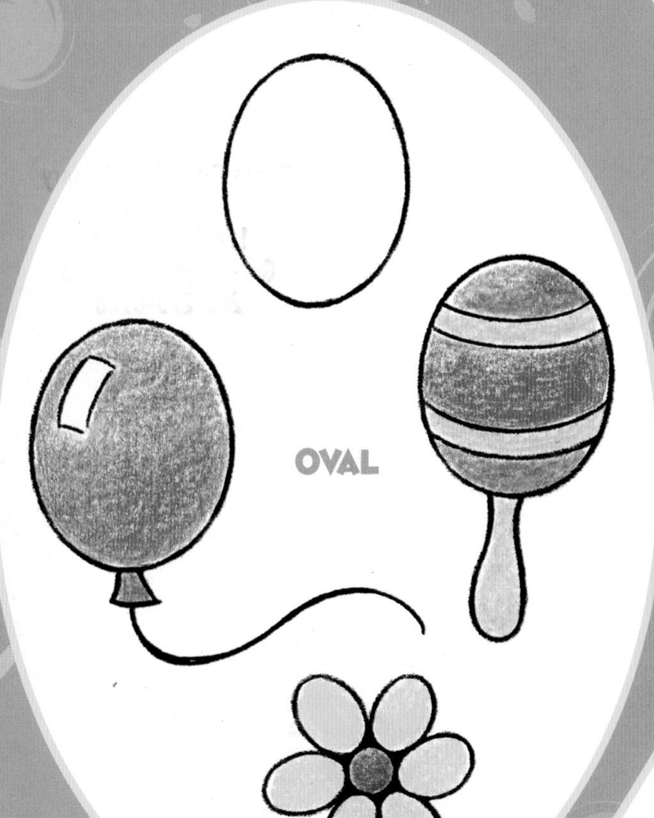

OVAL

TRIANGLE

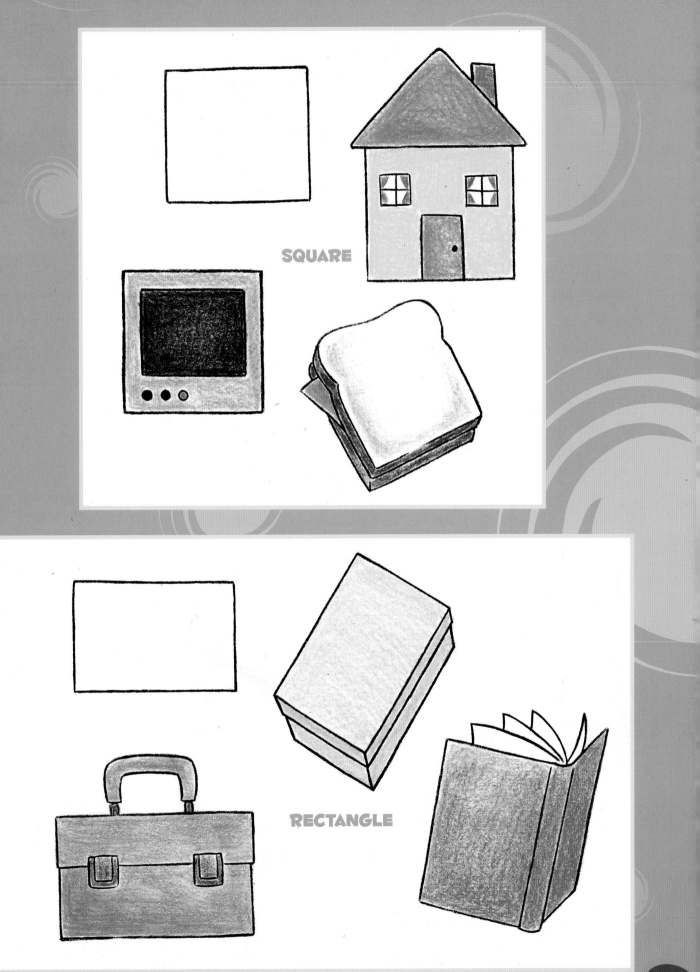

SQUARE

RECTANGLE

TIMMY

Timmy Turner is pretty smart, is highly imaginative, and has a short attention span. Basically he's your average 10-year-old boy . . . sort of. What's different about Timmy? When he says, "I wish," his Fairy Godparents grant it—even if they don't always hear him correctly!

YES! Timmy's hat follows the curve of his head

YES! Hat button floats

NO! Hat is not lower than hairline

NO! Hat button isn't attached

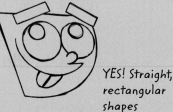

Timmy's (and Cosmo's) eyebrows don't curve

YES! Straight, rectangular shapes

NO! Not curved lines

STEP 1

Begin with the basic shape of Timmy's head; then add his triangular body and a guideline for his facial features. Next draw two ovals for his eyes and an upside-down "U" for his nose.

STEP 4

Finish drawing Timmy's hat, and then add the rest of his mouth—including his tongue and those front teeth! Draw the rest of his shirt and add the curlicue in his ear.

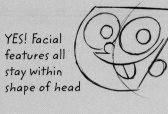
YES! Facial features all stay within shape of head

NO! Eyes and mouth should not extend beyond face

STEP 2

Now draw jagged lines to show the shape of Timmy's hair. Add two circles to his eyes and another circle for his ear. Then draw his arms and legs.

STEP 3

Next draw the curved lines of Timmy's big grin and connect the top line to his nose. Add his eyebrows, hands, and feet. Then draw the bottom part of his hat.

STEP 5

Now carefully erase any stray pencil lines. Then use the sharp point of your pencil or a fine-tip black marker to darken the outline.

STEP 6

Next use crayons, colored pencils, or markers to add some color, bringing Timmy to life!

COSMO

It's a good thing Timmy has not one, but two Fairy Godparents! Cosmo means well, but to be frank, most of the time he has no idea what he's doing in the magic department. But what he lacks in ability, he makes up for with his great sense of humor, boundless energy, and endless good mood.

When Cosmo (or Wanda) is floating at rest, the body has a simple shape and front leg fits within shape

YES! Crown floats above head and lines up with side of head

NO! Crown doesn't touch head or shift left

Godparents have pupils and noses that are more pointed than Timmy's

Godparents   Timmy

STEP 1

Start with the basic shape of Cosmo's head. Then draw some circles for his eyes and his ear. His body is shaped like an arrow!

STEP 4

Next refine Cosmo's hands and draw the rest of his wand and his wings. Finish off his crown. Then create the details on his mouth, ear, and shirt.

YES! Cosmo's tie has a straight end and always lies flat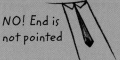

NO! End is not pointed

NO! Tie does not move

Next draw his hair and finish his eyes. Then add two pairs of straight lines under his chin for his arms and another straight line at his waist.

Now add Cosmo's expressive eyebrows and his charming grin. Add the shapes of his hands and refine his legs. Then draw the bottom of his crown and the star-shaped tip of his wand.

Erase all the guidelines you don't need. Then darken the ones you want to keep as outlines for your finished drawing.

Once you're happy with your drawing, all that's left is to color in Cosmo! Excellent work!

WANDA

Sure, Wanda is a bit on the zany side, but she's the most practical and capable half of Timmy's Godparent duo. Wanda loves using her "powers" to make things better, even if that means fixing one of Cosmo's slip-ups. But her major focus is on making sure that Timmy is happy and well taken care of.

Wanda's eyelashes extend past her head

When her mouth is closed, top and bottom lips don't line up

There are many different ways to show magical powers in action (you can even make up your own!)

STEP 1

As usual, you'll want to start with the basic shapes of Wanda's head and face. Just like Cosmo, she has an arrow-shaped body.

STEP 4

Next finish off Wanda's winning smile. Then add her long eyelashes and her wings. Give her some earrings and refine her crown and wand.

When Wanda or Cosmo are fish, they look identical except for face details

PLACE FACE HERE

STEP 2

Now refine her legs and eyes and add straight lines for her arms. Then add her hair—it's like the swirl of a cinnamon roll, and it sits at the front of her head.

STEP 3

Connect the curving lines of Wanda's smile to her nose; then draw her eyebrows and her hands. Don't forget to add her wand and the bottom of her crown!

STEP 5

Get rid of any lines you don't need. Then darken Wanda's outline, paying special attention to those long eyelashes, her crown, and the handle of her wand.

STEP 6

That's all there is to it! Now finish your drawing by coloring her with shades of bright pink and yellow.

SpongeBob SquarePants

SpongeBob lives in a fully furnished pineapple under the sea with his pet snail Gary. When he's not working hard at The Krusty Krab, he has a lot of interests that keep him occupied: jellyfishing, bubble art, and karate. His never-ending good nature and enthusiasm can often irritate others, but his refreshing attitude makes him a likable underdog. Despite all of his positive traits, "SpongeBob excitement" usually means "SpongeBob disaster." In the end, though, SpongeBob always wins—even if only for himself.

STEP 1

Start with the basic SpongeBob square. Lightly pencil in guidelines for his face and his clothes.

STEP 2

Next draw his features. Then add his arms, legs, hands, and feet. And don't forget his shoes, sleeves, and pant legs!

STEP 3

Now make the sponge edges wavy and finish SpongeBob's eyes. Then follow the blue lines to add all the rest of his spongy details.

SpongeBob's thick eyelashes start at the outer corners of his irises, but they show only above his eyeballs.

SpongeBob's prickly pineapple palace is a perfectly cozy underwater home.

Make SpongeBob's teeth big and square like this . . .

. . . not long and goofy like this.

STEP 5

Ta-da! Use crayons, markers, or colored pencils to finish SpongeBob with bright, bubbly colors—and don't forget his freckled cheeks!

STEP 4

To clean up your drawing, erase any lines you don't need.

When SpongeBob smiles, his cheeks are small and round, with three freckles.

Don't flatten out his cheeks like this.

Patrick Star

Patrick is SpongeBob's dim-witted yet loyal best friend. His hobbies include sleeping and lying still. This starfish truly idolizes SpongeBob, and together they make a mess of things for everyone around them—but always without meaning to. Part sloth and part dude, Patrick's biggest ambition in life is "uh . . . I . . . uh . . . forget."

When Patrick uses his hands, they look like mittens. Be sure to keep them very simple.

holding something

making a fist

pointing

waving good-bye

STEP 1

Patrick's eyebrows look like two thick "Z's" squished together . . .

. . . like this . . .

. . . not like this. Don't make them too thin!

STEP 2

Start with a big teardrop shape for Patrick's body. Then add the guidelines for his face and his shorts.

Draw rounded triangle shapes for his arms and legs. Then add his eyes and mouth.

Patrick's flowery pants look the same from the front and back. There's one large flower in the middle and one smaller flower on each side.

STEP 4

Now erase any pencil lines you don't need.

STEP 3

Follow the blue lines to add his trunks and the rest of the details on his face and body. Don't forget his belly button!

STEP 5

When Patrick is really angry or scared, he shows his round teeth!

Color Patrick's tropical trunks seaweed green. Then outline his body in red.

Squidward Tentacles

Co-worker and neighbor of SpongeBob, Squidward is a bitter and obnoxious octopus. Everyone and everything annoy him—except his own clarinet playing and painting. This could be because Squidward is two arms short of a full set of tentacles.

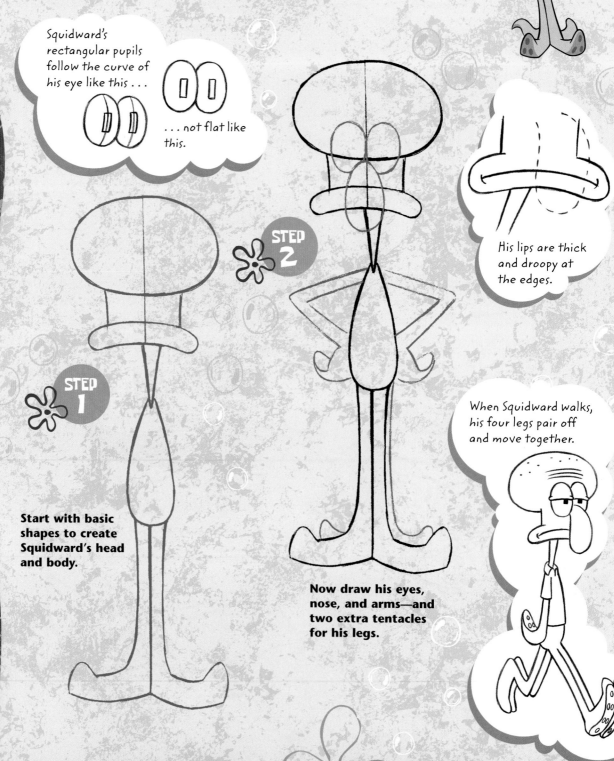

Squidward's rectangular pupils follow the curve of his eye like this . . .

. . . not flat like this.

His lips are thick and droopy at the edges.

STEP 1

Start with basic shapes to create Squidward's head and body.

STEP 2

Now draw his eyes, nose, and arms—and two extra tentacles for his legs.

When Squidward walks, his four legs pair off and move together.

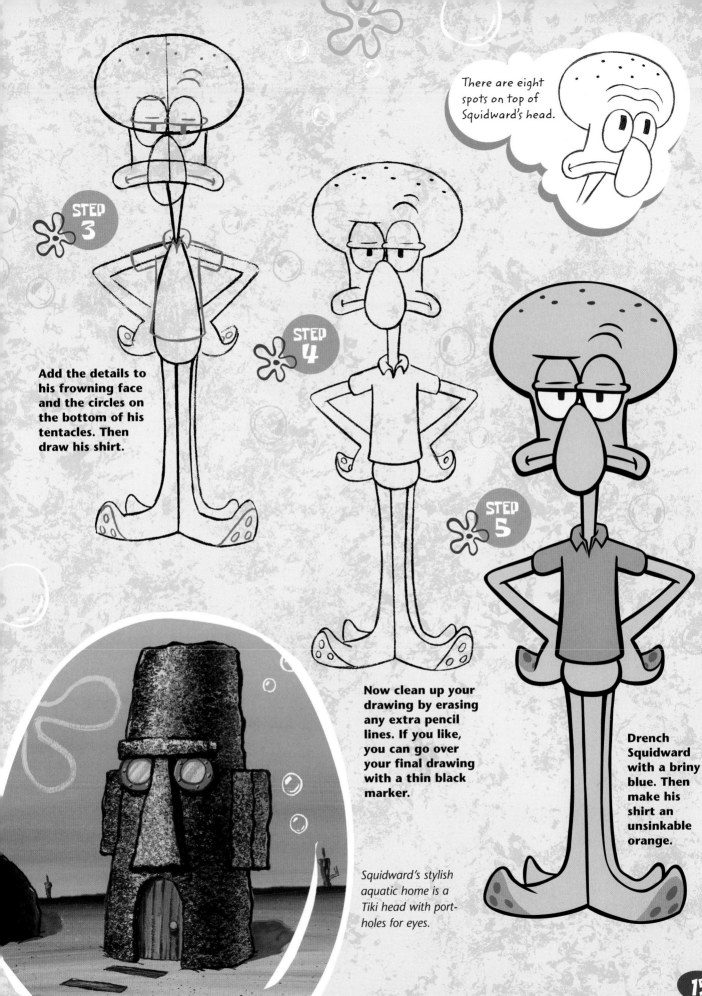

There are eight spots on top of Squidward's head.

Add the details to his frowning face and the circles on the bottom of his tentacles. Then draw his shirt.

Now clean up your drawing by erasing any extra pencil lines. If you like, you can go over your final drawing with a thin black marker.

Drench Squidward with a briny blue. Then make his shirt an unsinkable orange.

Squidward's stylish aquatic home is a Tiki head with port-holes for eyes.

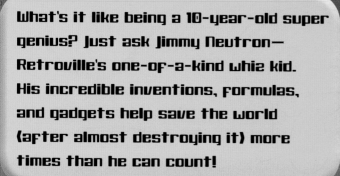

JIMMY NEUTRON

What's it like being a 10-year-old super genius? Just ask Jimmy Neutron—Retroville's one-of-a-kind whiz kid. His incredible inventions, formulas, and gadgets help save the world (after almost destroying it) more times than he can count!

STEP 2

Now outline his eyes, nose, and mouth. Draw cylinders for his arms and legs and circles for his hands. Then add the shapes of his shoes and a line for his belt.

STEP 1

Start with an egg shape and an oval for Jimmy's head. Then add an upside-down egg shape for his body.

Think of Jimmy's head as a dollop of whipped cream on top of a light bulb inside of a doughnut

Jimmy's hair changes shape in reaction to extreme movements

Jimmy's chest symbol looks like Saturn, with 3 rings.

STEP 3

Add the details to his face and outline the shape of his hair. Next draw his fingers and erase the extra guidelines on his face.

STEP 4

Draw the hairline around his face and the curlicues in his ears. Then refine the lines of his hands. Next draw the shapes of his shirt, pants, and shoes.

STEP 5

Next add the design on his shirt and clean up your drawing by erasing any extra pencil lines.

STEP 6

Now finish your drawing of Jimmy by coloring him in. That's all there is to it!

CARL WHEEZER

Carl is allergic to . . . well, just about everything—which means that even breathing can be a pretty big challenge for him. But even so, Jimmy's best friend (and scientific guinea pig) comes along for every adventure . . . after voicing his reservations, of course.

STEP 1

Carl's head and body are shaped like two big circles with a square hat on top. Don't forget to add guidelines for his face, pants, and buttons.

STEP 2

Add his round glasses, his mouth, and the shapes of his arms, hands, legs, and feet.

Carl's suspenders crisscross over his back

Carl's hair looks like teardrops sprouting from the top of his head

Carl's knees are usually bent

STEP 3

Fill in his features and draw ovals for his hair. Add fingers and a squiggle for his pants.

STEP 4

Add the details to his face and ears. Refine his hands and shoes and outline his shirt, suspenders, and pants.

STEP 5

Next just add the stripes on Carl's shirt and erase any guidelines you have left over.

STEP 6

Now all you have to do is color him in, and your drawing's complete!

CINDY VORTEX

Certain that she's just as smart as Jimmy is, Cindy's mission is to convince the rest of Retroville that she's not the second-smartest Retroville resident. But the constant competition between these two brainiacs produces some seriously sticky situations!

Cindy's fingers are smaller and thinner than Jimmy's and Carl's

Boy's hand

Girl's hand

STEP 2

Add the swoop of her bangs and the outlines of her facial features. Draw the shapes of her arms, legs, and feet, and place her hands on her hips.

STEP 1

Start Cindy's saucy stance with a large egg shape and an oval for her head and a bean shape for her body.

Cindy's eyelashes are made with a thick outline across her eye

Without his hair, Jimmy is shorter than Cindy!

STEP 4

Now add eyebrows and refine her ears, hands, and shoes. Then draw the outlines of her socks, shirt, and pants.

STEP 3

Complete the outline of her hair and add the curl of her ponytail. Draw her ear and finish her eyes. Then add the soles of her shoes and her curved fingers.

STEP 6

Ta-da! Now finish your drawing of Cindy with a zing of color!

STEP 5

Next draw two curved lines on her shirt and an extra line on each pant leg. Then erase any guidelines you haven't already removed.

ROCKET POWER

Otto Rocket

Otto is the fearless leader of the Rocket Power gang. To say that he's obsessed with sports would be an understatement. And sometimes his endless pursuit of athletic perfection can make him a little unreliable (okay, a lot).

Step 1

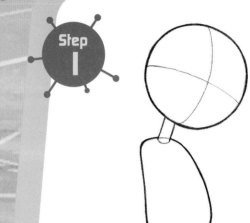

Begin Otto with a circle and a squarish bean shape connected by a cylinder.

Otto's eyes are shaped a little like kidney beans

Otto's hair is in the shape of a hot dog but with lumps on both sides

Otto's clothing is always very wrinkled

Step 4

Add glasses and squiggle the outlines of his hair and clothes. Then erase the guidelines.

Step 2

Place his eyes and headband. Then add the shapes of his arms, legs, hands, and feet.

Step 3

Outline his hair, face, features, clothes and shoes. Then draw straight fingers.

Step 5

Draw details on his glasses and rumpled clothes, and fill in his toothy grin.

Step 6

That's it! Now just grab your colors to finish your rad drawing of Otto!

Twister

Twister is always there for Otto—after all, that's what best friends are for. Twister is the daredevil of the group— and also the cameraman. He never goes anywhere without his handheld video cam, which he uses to film the gang's extreme sports adventures.

Step 1

Twister's basic shapes look a lot like Otto's but with a slightly smaller head.

Twister's eyes are partially covered by his hat

Twister's hair sticks out the front of his hat in the shape of fire

Step 4

Make wavy outlines and add details to his face and shoes. Then erase any extra lines.

Step **2**

Step **3**

Outline his eyes and hat. Then add the shapes of his hands, feet, and limbs.

Draw his features and hair; then outline his face and clothes. Draw his fingers.

Step **5**

Step **6**

Add the finishing details and refine all your lines. Don't forget the pockets!

Now color him in, and Twister is ready to roll!

Reggie & Sam

Reggie is Otto's sister. More than just an awesome athlete, this girl hero publishes her own 'zine, which covers everything from sports to kid politics. Sam is the new kid in town, and he is the voice of Rocket Power reason. This New York native is smart, questioning, and cautious, and he keeps the group grounded.

The design on Reggie's pants is flower shaped

Sam's eyes are exactly 1 eye-width apart

Step 1

Block in all the basic shapes, starting with a circle for Reggie's head.

Step 1

Sam is wide and his clothes are blocky, so use big shapes and a rounded square for his head.

Step 2

Start drawing his glasses and features. Then outline his clothes and draw his hands and the soles of his shoes.

Step
2

Step
3

Step
4

Outline her features and the shapes of her hair and clothes. Add curved lines on her pants.

Wiggle the outlines and add the details to her face. Refine the lines of the pants pattern.

Make sure all the guidelines are erased. Then color Reggie as boldly as you like!

Step
3

Step
4

Use wavy lines for the outlines of his clothes. Then erase all the guidelines and add the finishing details.

Now color him in! (Notice that the hand closest to you looks bigger than the other. That's called *foreshortening!*)

TOMMY PICKLES

Tommy is a born leader. He's smart, loves adventure, and has a special way of charming others (grownups and babies alike). Tommy runs the show—and convinces the others that "a baby's gotta do what a baby's gotta do."

STEP 2

STEP 1

Add the curve of his mouth and ovals for his eyes. Then block in the shapes of his arms, hands, legs, and feet.

Start drawing Tommy with a circle for his head and a bean shape for his body. Add guidelines for his face.

Tommy has 7 tiny hairs

Tommy's fingers look a lot like mini sausages

STEP 3

Next draw the bumpy outline of his head and face and add his pupils. Draw hands and feet and outline his clothes.

STEP 4

Add his tongue and refine all your outlines, making his diaper look bunchy. Then erase all the guidelines.

STEP 5

Now add the details that make Tommy unique, like the little hairs on his head and the dimples on his knees.

STEP 6

When you've finished adding all the details (don't forget his belly button!), all that's left is to color him in!

CHUCKIE FINSTER

Part worrywart and part fraidy cat, Chuckie is one nervous little guy. This stuffy-nosed tot is the Rugrats' voice of caution. The Rugrats can always count on Chuckie to warn everyone about the dangers of, well, everything!

STEP 2

Add square eyes, oval pupils, a round nose and ear, and a wide grin. Then draw the shapes of his arms, legs, hands, and feet.

STEP 1

Chuckie begins with a circle for his head and a bean shape for his body. Connect them with a small cylinder.

Chuckie's hair looks like candle flames

Chuckie's freckles form a triangle shape

STEP 3

Start his hair with spikes and add square glasses. Outline his clothes and draw his hands and shoes.

STEP 4

Now make those spikes wavy and add a rectangle for his teeth. Refine the outlines of his clothes and add details.

STEP 5

Next add the details to his face and clothes, including his undone shoe-laces. Don't leave off his freckles!

STEP 6

Chuckie's complete! All he needs is a little color to bring him to life, and he's ready for more adventures!

ANGELICA PICKLES

Angelica is the bossy 3-year old responsible for bringing the Rugrats together. But this know-it-all is also a pigtailed super-threat who believes babies were born so she could pick on them, trick them, and blame them for things they didn't do!

STEP 2

Then draw triangles for pigtails and circles for eyes. Add the curves of her cheek and ear and shape her limbs.

STEP 1

Like all the Rugrats, Angelica starts out as a circle-shaped head, a bean-shaped body, and a cylindrical neck.

Angelica's dress resembles a wide-brimmed hat

Angelica's eyes each have 4 lashes